DK SUPERGUIDES
GOLF

Written by Richard Simmons
Foreword by Nick Faldo

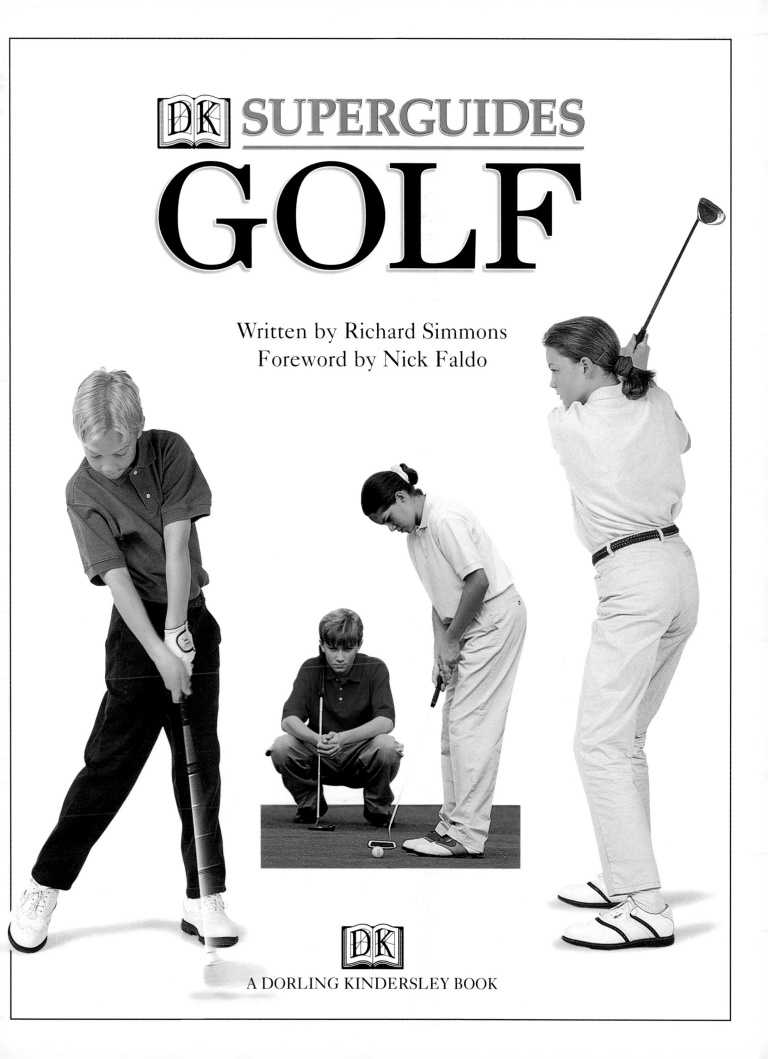

DK

A DORLING KINDERSLEY BOOK

Dorling DK Kindersley

LONDON, NEW YORK, SYDNEY, DELHI, PARIS,
MUNICH and JOHANNESBURG

Project Editor Selina Wood **Designer** Jacqueline Gooden
Managing Editor Mary Ling
Managing Art Editor Rachael Foster
Digital Artwork Robin Hunter
Consultant Nigel Blenkarne
Photography Steve Gorton, Andrew Redington
DTP Designer Almudena Díaz
Picture Research Angela Anderson
Production Lisa Moss and Kenneth McKay
US Editor Constance Robinson
US Consultant Don Wade

The young golfers
Clare Blenkarne, Nicholas Blenkarne, Phelps Brooks, Mary Calderon,
Daniela Díaz, Amy Swales, Matthew Swales

First American Edition, 2001

00 01 02 03 04 05 10 9 8 7 6 5 4 3 2 1

Published in the United States by
Dorling Kindersley Publishing, Inc.
95 Madison Avenue
New York, NY 10016

ISBN 0-7894-7390-9

Color reproduction by Colourscan, Singapore
Printed and bound in Italy by L.E.G.O.

See our complete
catalog at
www.dk.com

Contents

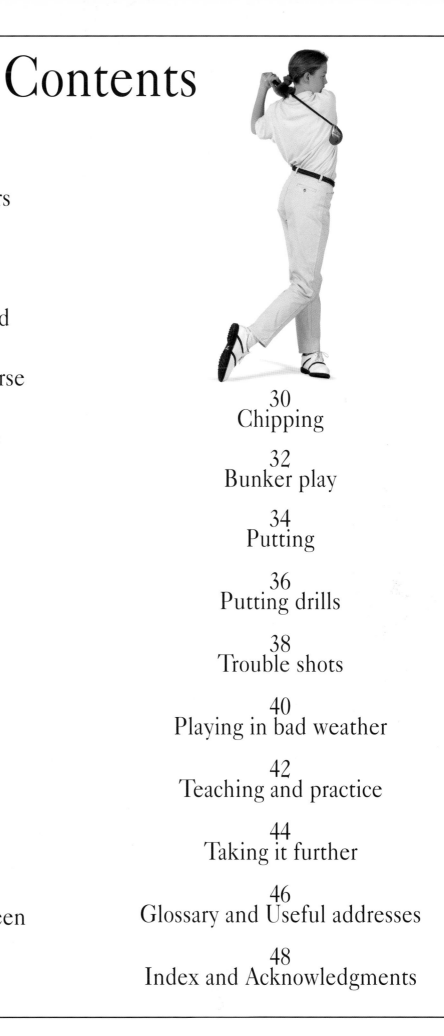

To all young golfers

"I CAN STILL REMEMBER the moment I decided to be a golfer. Watching television, I caught a glimpse of Jack Nicklaus playing in the 1971 Masters tournament at Augusta National. I was 13 years old. Before long every spare minute of the day was spent playing and reading about golf. In 1975, I became the youngest-ever winner of the English Amateur Championship. As you are about to discover, golf is a lifelong education. There are no shortcuts to success – the path of professional instruction and regular practice is the only way forward. The lessons in this book will set you on your way to a long and rewarding experience. Enjoy the game and the many rewards it holds in store."

"Here I am holding the British Open Trophy after victory at Muirfield in 1992."

"I have always loved to practice! As an amateur in the 1970s I worked very hard."

"In 1987, I had my sights on a first major championship win at Muirfield."

"Representing Europe in the Ryder Cup matches has been one of the highlights of my career."

"At Augusta National in 1996, there was drama all the way to the final hole as I won my third Masters title."

Medieval and Renaissance games

In medieval and Renaissance times, there were several ball-and-club games played in northern Europe. This illustration, from a Flemish *Book of Hours* (1530), shows people playing a game similar to modern golf.

History of golf

THE ORIGINS OF GOLF are unclear. It may have started as *Paganica*, a game introduced to Britain by the Romans, or as a ball-and-club game played in medieval Europe known as *kolf*. The game we know today evolved in Scotland, where its great popularity gave rise to the formation of groups of players, or clubs, in the 18th century. The first major tournament – the British Open – was held in 1860. By the turn of the century, golf was growing in popularity worldwide, especially in the US.

Golf rules

In 1744, Duncan Forbes, the first captain of the Gentleman Golfers of Leith, Scotland, was one of the first people to create golf rules. In 1897, the Royal and Ancient Golf Club of St. Andrews compiled a uniform code of rules.

Early equipment

Early golf balls were fragile objects made of leather and filled with goose feathers. They were superseded by harder and cheaper "gutties" – balls made from a rubberlike substance found in the tropical percha tree. Until the 19th century, clubs were made of wood, and had longer faces than today's clubs.

Feather ball c. 1840

Guttie c. 1890

19th-century long-nosed woods

Cecil Leitch was a famous player in Britain between 1914 and 1926.

Bobby Jones

Bobby Jones's amateur record has never been beaten. In 1930, the American golfer achieved the "Grand Slam," winning both the Amateur and the professional Open Championships of Britain and the US.

The US Open Championship trophy

Tees

Tees were originally made of wood. Brightly colored so that they are easy to see in the grass, tees are now occasionally made of plastic.

Women's golf

Women first formed golf clubs in the late 19th century, and the first amateur tournaments took place in the 1890s. Women's golf made a major advance in 1949, with the formation of the Ladies' Professional Golf Association in the US.

The "Majors"

There are four major professional golf championships; the Open Championships of Britain and the US, the Masters Tournament, and the PGA Championship.

Jack Nicklaus

America's Jack Nicklaus is widely acknowledged as the best player the game has ever known. He has won 18 major championships: a record six Masters, four US Opens, five PGA Championships, and three British Opens.

Welcome to the course

GOLF IS PLAYED on a large expanse of grass known as a course. A full course has 18 areas, or holes, that pose different problems for the players. All holes have a teeing ground, a fairway, and a green. Hazards, such as sand bunkers, are positioned around each hole to make the game more difficult. The object of the game is to use clubs to hit the ball from the teeing ground to the hole on the green with the lowest number of strokes. Golf is usually played by groups of two to four people who move around the course together, each person taking a turn to play the ball.

The links course at Ballybunion, Ireland

Links and parkland courses

There are different types of golf courses. Links courses, such as St. Andrews, Scotland, are typically situated on land reclaimed from the sea. They have large sand dunes that come into play and are well open to the elements. Parkland courses, such as Augusta National in Georgia, contain trees and shrubs as part of the course's design.

The course

Each hole on a golf course is given a rating depending on its length. This rating, called "par," is the number of strokes an expert player would be expected to take to complete the hole. The illustration opposite shows a typical par-4, 420-yard hole with features and hazards. The red line indicates a route that might be taken by a top player, completing the hole in three strokes (one stroke under par). The blue line shows a route most likely to be taken by a beginner. This is not the most direct route, but a safer one that avoids hazards.

Augusta National

The Augusta National Golf Club in Georgia, is the home of the Masters tournament. It is a magnificent parkland course, famous for its immaculate condition and the notorious Amen Corner (holes 11, 12, and 13) where the Masters is often won or lost.

Teeing ground

Golfers play the first shot of each hole from the teeing ground. Markers indicate where to take the shot. Ladies have their own tee, which is forward of the men's, while a third "Championship" tee is used in competitions.

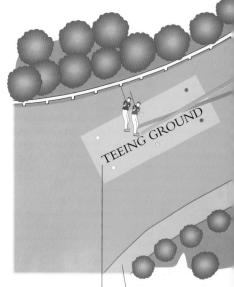

The teeing ground is the smooth, level area where you make your first stroke.

The water-filled ditch is a major hazard on this course.

St. Andrews

Golf has been played on the old links course at St. Andrews, Scotland, for over 400 years. Avoiding the bunkers is the key to survival around the course. There are dozens of them, and most of them are hidden from view.

Ditches

When architects design courses, they make imaginative use of hazards to capture wayward balls. Hazards (also known as "trouble") come in many forms, from sand bunkers to trees and gaping, water-filled ditches.

Bunkers

Bunkers are indented areas filled with sand. They are distributed on fairways and areas around the green. Many players fear a ball landing in a sand bunker, although some players find it easier to control a shot from a bunker than from deep grass.

Green

The ultimate target is to reach the hole, which can be situated almost anywhere on the green. Greens can vary in size and are rarely completely flat. The grass on the green is cut short to allow a smooth, fast roll of the ball.

The fairway is the area of mown grass where your second and third shots should be played. Shots landing in longer grass off the fairway are in the "rough."

Any shots that go beyond the out-of-bounds line must be replayed and also incur a penalty stroke.

The fringe or apron is the area surrounding the green.

BUNKER

GREEN

This is a direct route most likely to be played by skilled players.

FAIRWAY

BUNKER

The best beginner's route has extra distance but is safer.

Fairway

The area between the tee and the green is known as the fairway. It is a closely mown area surrounded by long grass or "rough" and can occasionally contain hazards. The fairway is where your second and third shots are normally played.

Yardage chart

Many golf courses have their own yardage charts. These detailed maps of each hole on the course provide players with all the information needed to plot a safe route from tee to green, avoiding hazards. Distances in yards are given from various points on the course. Once you have practiced, and know how far you can carry the ball with each type of club, the distances given on the charts will help you select the right club for each shot.

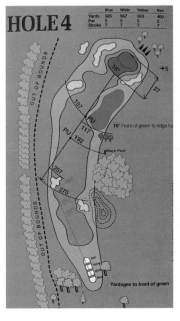

HOLE 4

	Blue	White	Yellow	Red
Yards	585	567	563	460
Par	5	5	5	5
Stroke	7	7	7	7

OUT OF BOUNDS

→5

18'

27

107

PU

117

PU

192

18' Front of green to ridge top

Black Post

257

270

OUT OF BOUNDS

Yardages to front of green

Playing the game

Y OU MAY BE EAGER to get onto the course, but before you play, it is important to understand the rules of the game, methods of scoring, and ways of assessing your ability. You should also observe the rules of etiquette, since you are likely to be sharing the course with several other players.

Scoring

Two of the most common scoring systems are the Medal system and the Stableford system. All scoring is based on the number of strokes taken by a player to complete a hole, compared to the "par" for that hole (see p. 8). The par rating for each hole depends on its length (shown in the table, right). Scorecards present this information in the form of a table, and have separate columns for the players' scores to be entered during a round. At the end of play, each scorecard is checked and signed by both players.

First swap cards, then mark your own score here, and the other player's score in the "A" column.

A selection of tee lengths is shown here.

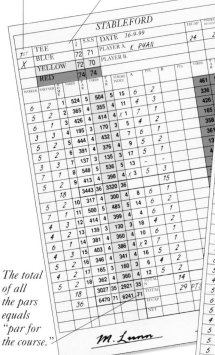

The total of all the pars equals "par for the course."

Medal system

The most widely used system of scoring in golf is known as Medal or Strokeplay. Under this format the total number of strokes a player takes to complete each hole is marked on the card. The player with the least number of strokes at the end of the round is the winner. A player's handicap (see the table, right) is deducted to determine the net (final) score for the round.

The player's score has come to a gross total of 92. On deducting the 21 handicap, the net score is 71.

The stroke index indicates the difficulty of each hole (18 is the easiest).

Stableford system

The Stableford system is a popular alternative to the Medal system. The Stableford format awards points for the number of strokes (net) taken at each hole. One point is awarded for a hole completed in one over par (for example, scoring a 6 on a par-5), two points are awarded for a hole played in par, three points for one under par (known as a "birdie"), and so on.

The Rules of Golf

Obtain a copy of the Rules of Golf, formalized by the US Golf Association and the Royal and Ancient Golf Club of St. Andrews, Scotland, to make yourself aware of the basic rules that govern play. There are 34 different rules: They include information on penalty shots and what to do when balls are hit into awkward places. They give you a clear guide as to how to settle common disputes that may occur during a round of golf.

Hole ratings

MEN
Hole length:
Up to 250 yd = par-3
251–475 yd = par-4
Over 476 yd = par-5

WOMEN
Hole length:
Up to 220 yd = par-3
220–430 yd = par-4
Over 409 yd = par-5

The handicap system

The handicap system enables players of varying levels of ability to compete against one another. Your handicap is based on the number of strokes by which you normally exceed the rating (par) of the course. This may be calculated from the average score of 3 games, played over the same course with a player who already possesses a handicap. The maximum handicap is 28 for a man and 45 for a woman. Nowadays, many clubs use computers that calculate and record scores after each round of golf – so handicaps tend to go up and down, depending on how a golfer is playing. Many clubs adopt special handicap systems for juniors, which go up to 48.

Scoring terms

The same as par = making par
One stroke under par = birdie
Two strokes under par = eagle
Three strokes under par = double-eagle
One stroke over par = bogey
Two strokes over par = double-bogey

Etiquette

Etiquette is an important part of the game; points of etiquette are noted in Section 1 of the Rules of Golf. This section describes common courtesy to other players and care of the course. You must not move or talk when others are playing, or stand where you may distract a player's concentration. In the interests of other golfers you should try to play without delay. If a member of your group loses a ball that is not quickly found, call any players behind to pass you and play on.

Carefully rake your footprints as you leave the bunker.

Pitch-mark tool

Repairing pitch marks

All players should take responsibility for care of the course. Approach shots to the green often leave a pitch mark where the ball lands. These indentations should be carefully repaired using a pitch-mark tool. Lift the turf with the prongs of the fork and gently tap down the surface of the green with the bottom of your putter.

Make sure you repair all divots immediately.

Raking the bunker

After each visit to a bunker you should rake the sand carefully to smooth out your footprints and any other marks that you have created. Leave a bunker as you would want to find it – there is usually a rake available on the course.

Divot marks

When you play a shot, particularly with an iron club, the impact can remove a shallow cut of turf, known as a divot. To keep the course in good condition, put the divot back in the ground, pressing it down firmly with your foot.

Quietly stand to one side while a player tees off.

Shaking hands

At the end of a round it is traditional to shake hands with your playing partners and thank them for the game. Win or lose, there should be no hard feelings as you leave the course.

Make sure people are standing clear when you strike.

Safety

Safety on the course is the responsibility of all golfers. Prior to playing a stroke or making a practice swing, be sure that no one is standing in a position to be hit by a club or the ball. If you hit a ball that flies in the direction of other players you should warn them of the danger by shouting "Fore!"

Preparing to play

BEFORE YOU PLAY or practice golf you should spend a few minutes limbering up. This helps prevent injury by warming up and stretching the muscles that you will need to make a good swing.

Leg stretch

This exercise will help you stretch out and strengthen your calf and thigh muscles. From a standing position, take a big stride forward, bending your front knee. Place you hands on your knee, and hold this position for a count of three. Repeat the stretch, placing your opposite leg forward.

Keep your back straight and your head up.

Your rear foot is balanced on the toe of the shoe.

Your weight should be supported on your front foot.

Feel the stretch in both legs as you hold the position.

Your back knee should not touch the ground.

Arm stretch

In preparation for making a full shoulder turn when you swing your club, you should stretch the muscles in your arms and shoulders.

Pull your left arm across your chest.

1 To start, hook your right arm under your left, then pull your left arm tight across your chest. Gently press your left arm back with your right arm.

Turn your body in the same direction as your straight arm.

Flex your knees for balance.

Let your head turn with your shoulders.

2 Pull your left arm and left shoulder to the right to stretch the muscles in your upper body. Hold this position for a count of three, then repeat the stretch to the opposite side.

Pivot exercise

This pivot stretch is one of the most effective warm-up and flexibility exercises for the golf swing. It helps you to develop a supple spine for a full shoulder turn.

Hold the club horizontally on your shoulders.

Place your hands at either end of the club.

Keep your head up as you turn.

1 Stand with your feet shoulder-width apart; bend forward slightly from the hips. Hook a club across the back of your shoulders.

Feel the muscles in your torso stretch.

Your right knee should remain flexed.

Bend your knees, ready to support the turning motion.

2 Turn your shoulders and upper body as far as you can to the right. Feel your weight shift onto your right side.

Move your left knee gently toward the right.

Keep your feet still with your heels firmly on the ground.

Rotation exercise

The basic golf swing involves a rotation of the upper body. To warm up and stretch the muscles used in this rotary movement, complete this exercise before you start playing.

Ease your head to the right to assist your turn.

Keep your arms straight.

Your left arm crosses your chest.

2 Shift your weight onto your left side as you rotate your body. Repeat the exercise three more times.

The arms swing as you turn your body.

1 Grip the shaft of a club, placing your hands shoulder-width apart.

Hold the clubhead slightly above the ground.

Wrist exercise

A good wrist action is essential for all golf strokes. Work on improving the flexibility and the mobility of your wrists with this simple exercise.

2 Move your wrists upwards and downward to raise and lower the clubhead. Sense the control in your hands and fingers.

Your back should remain straight.

1 Grip the club shaft and hold the club in front of your body. Keep your grip light so that the muscles in your hands and arms remain relaxed.

Keep your elbows close to your body.

Your head turns naturally with your shoulders.

3 Hold the position for a count of 10, then repeat the exercise to the left. Repeat twice more to each side.

Your knees are close together at the finish.

Let your heel come off the ground.

Swing two clubs

Swinging two iron clubs together in slow motion is another good warm-up exercise. The extra weight of the clubs will help you swing smoothly and strengthen your muscles.

1 Start with your feet shoulder-width apart. Hold two clubs together and swing them over one shoulder.

Bend your knee as you twist your upper body.

The two clubs finish together, angled behind you.

Exercise routine
A simple exercise program of 10 minutes a day will help improve your golf.

The weight of the two clubs stretches the muscles in your upper body.

2 Let the weight of the two clubs pull your arms back over your shoulder. Hold this position for a count of three. Repeat twice more to each side.

Bring your knees together as you turn.

Your heel should come off the ground.

Powerful grip
A good grip enables you to transfer the power of your swing accurately to the ball at impact. This skill is effortlessly displayed by Jack Nicklaus, who uses the interlocking grip.

Left-handed golfers
All golf instructions in this book are for right-handed golfers. Try holding a mirror alongside these pictures to see the left-handed positions.

Wrist action
The test of a good grip is that it enables the two hands to work together as a unit, and also that it allows the wrists to cock smoothly during the course of making the swing. The muscles in your hands and arms should always feel supple. It is a good idea to check your grip regularly.

The last three fingers on the left hand and the middle two on the right hand take the most pressure.

The golf grip

AS YOUR ONLY POINT of contact with the club, a good grip is vital for golf. The position of your hands on the club determines how well you are able to cock your wrists to make an effective swing. Your grip also affects the position of the clubface as it makes contact with the ball – most shots that curve to the right or left are the result of a bad grip. Use this step-by-step guide to position your hands correctly.

Elements of the grip

There are a number of ways in which you can join your hands together to form a good grip. The majority of top players use what is known as the Vardon grip, in which the little finger on the right hand overlaps the index finger on the left. Other players – particularly those with small hands – prefer to interlock their fingers. Try out different grips to decide which one works best for you. Just remember to grip the club gently at all times, so that your hands and arms stay relaxed.

2 When you look down at your left hand, at least two-and-a-half knuckles should be visible. Your left thumb sits on top of the shaft.

1 Grip the club low in the fingers of your left hand as if you were picking up a hammer. Sit the club in the crook of your forefinger.

Starting position
Rest the club at the top of your right leg. From here, take the club into your left hand. You will now be in the correct position for the grip.

Relax your shoulders.

Let your arms hang naturally before you pick up the club.

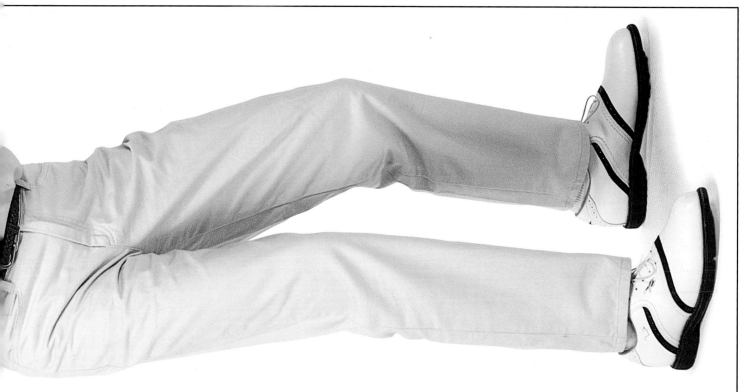

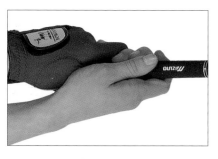

5 Your two hands are now comfortably joined and can work together. It is best to grip lightly for good flexibility.

Baseball grip
The baseball grip, in which the two hands sit side by side on the club, is a good "starter grip" for very young players. Use the Vardon or interlocking grip as you develop more strength.

4 The fleshy pad at the base of your right thumb should cover your left thumb as your hands are joined together.

Interlocking grip
Entwining the little finger on the right hand with the forefinger on the left results in an interlocking grip, popular with players who have small hands and fingers.

3 Bring in your right hand so that it fits snugly against the left. The club should rest in the channel formed by bending your middle two fingers.

The Vardon grip
The Vardon (or overlapping) grip was popularized by the British golfer Harry Vardon. The little finger on the right hand sits in the groove between the first and second fingers on the left hand.

Setup

THE STARTING POSITION from which you make your swing is known as the address, or setup. At the setup, you need to make sure your body, the clubface, and the ball are aligned. This is important for three reasons. Your body alignment determines the direction of your swing, your posture dictates the shape of your swing, and the ball always travels in line with the angle of the clubface.

Ball and feet position

Depending on what club you use to play a shot, your foot and ball positions will change slightly. For long clubs (woods), place the ball opposite the inside of the left heel, with your feet shoulder-width apart. Move the ball a little farther back toward the right foot for long irons (3-, 4-) and mid-irons (5-, 6-, 7-), and to the middle of your stance for the shorter and more lofted clubs (8-, 9-, and pitching wedge).

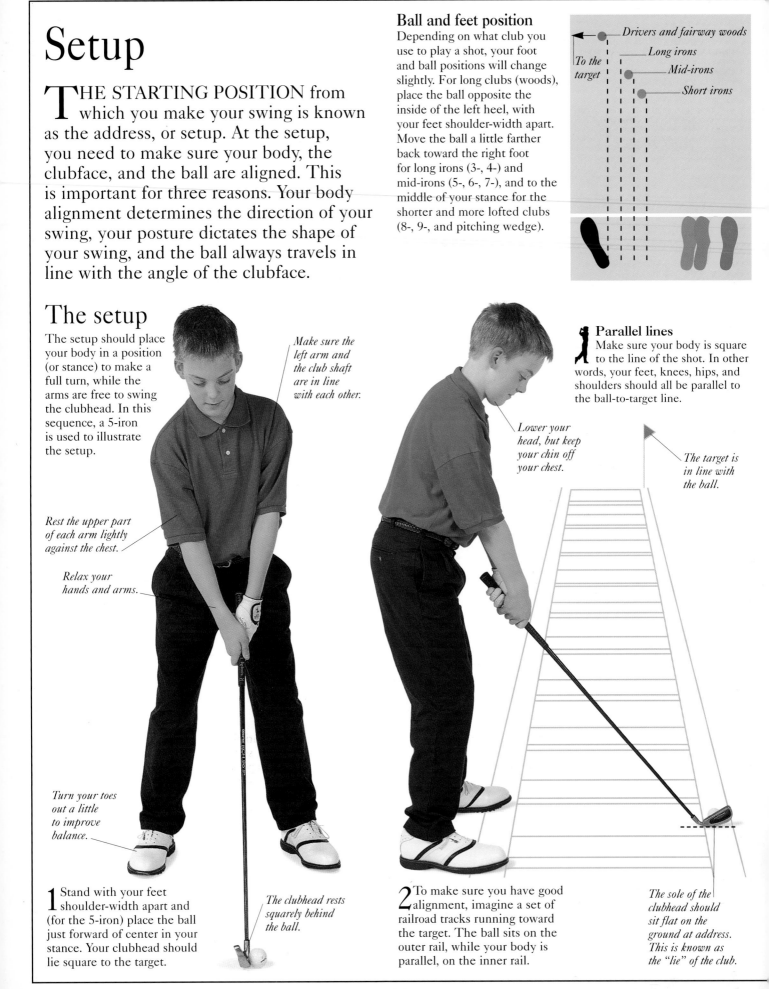

Drivers and fairway woods

To the target

Long irons

Mid-irons

Short irons

The setup

The setup should place your body in a position (or stance) to make a full turn, while the arms are free to swing the clubhead. In this sequence, a 5-iron is used to illustrate the setup.

Make sure the left arm and the club shaft are in line with each other.

Rest the upper part of each arm lightly against the chest.

Relax your hands and arms.

Turn your toes out a little to improve balance.

1 Stand with your feet shoulder-width apart and (for the 5-iron) place the ball just forward of center in your stance. Your clubhead should lie square to the target.

The clubhead rests squarely behind the ball.

Parallel lines

Make sure your body is square to the line of the shot. In other words, your feet, knees, hips, and shoulders should all be parallel to the ball-to-target line.

Lower your head, but keep your chin off your chest.

The target is in line with the ball.

2 To make sure you have good alignment, imagine a set of railroad tracks running toward the target. The ball sits on the outer rail, while your body is parallel, on the inner rail.

The sole of the clubhead should sit flat on the ground at address. This is known as the "lie" of the club.

Perfect posture

Good posture at address encourages you to make a good turn – or pivot motion – as you swing. Work hard at getting it right and you are more likely to achieve a consistent swing. This exercise will help you gain perfect posture with whatever club you are using.

Posture tip
Good golfers bend from the hips – never the waist. This allows the spine to remain straight so that it can rotate easily.

Make sure your arms are straight.

Your head should remain steady.

Keep your back straight when you bend your knees.

Bend forward from the hips.

1 To start, stand up straight, with your feet spread shoulder-width apart, and hold the club out comfortably just above waist height.

2 Gently bend forward from your hips and lower your arms until the clubhead rests on the ground. Do not alter the relationship between your arms and body.

3 Flex your knees and sense that your weight is centered on the balls of your feet. Spend a few seconds settling your feet. The correct posture should create a "bouncy" feeling.

Keep your feet flat on the ground.

Balance your weight equally on both legs.

The feet, knees, hips, and shoulders are parallel to the target line.

Pre-shot routine

A pre-shot routine helps you prepare mentally for a shot. Think of aiming the clubface at your target and placing your body in the correct position over the ball.

The waggle
To keep your arms and hands free of tension, move the club back-and-forth a few times before you swing. This is known as the "waggle."

Focus on the target as you waggle.

Start with your perfect posture routine.

Relax your shoulders.

Keep focusing on the target.

1 Always stand behind the ball to get a good look at the target. Focus on the type of shot you need to play and visualize the flight of the ball in your mind's eye.

2 Place your club on the ground and carefully aim the clubface. Check that the bottom edge is aligned squarely with your target.

3 Once you are satisfied with your aim, settle your body into position. Make sure your lower body is parallel with the target line.

Step forward to place your club.

The clubface is looking at the target.

The swing

TO CREATE A FREE-FLOWING swing, you must learn to blend the motion of your hands and arms with the turn of your body as you shift your body weight. Think of the swing as one continuous motion, from the setup to the finish, that strikes the ball along the way.

Elements of the swing

The two sequences on this page show the swing from the front and from the side. They will help you understand the key positions in a good swing. However, it is important to focus on swinging the club through these positions in one smooth movement; a good rhythm is the secret to good ball-striking. Make sure you grip the club lightly to enable your wrists to cock naturally as you move the clubhead in a wide, circular motion.

The club should be parallel to the target line.

1 Bend forward from the hips and gently flex the knees to create a good athletic posture at address. Keep your back straight and your shoulders relaxed.

Keep your eyes focused on the ball.

Make sure your hands and arms are relaxed.

The right knee is flexed, supporting the backswing.

2 To make the backswing, turn your upper body away from the target, and keep your lower body facing forward. For a full swing, turn your shoulders about 90°.

The shoulders are relaxed, ready to turn in the backswing.

Hold your chin up and away from your chest.

2 The takeaway is the moment you lift the club away from the ball. For a smooth movement, your arms and the club should work as a unit. Keep the clubhead close to the ground.

Cock your wrists so that the shaft is parallel to the ball-to-target line.

3 The backswing lifts the club above your head. Turn your upper body away from the ball, leaving your left shoulder under your chin and most of your weight on the right leg.

1 A good setup enables you to make an effective swing. Let your arms hang comfortably from your shoulders.

Your left arm should be straight to make your swing wide.

Flex your knees to keep you balanced.

Keep the clubhead low to the ground as you move it away from the ball.

Most of your weight is supported by your right leg.

SETUP

TAKEAWAY

BACKSWING

3 Unwind your body toward the target, so that the clubhead accelerates into the ball at speed.

Your arms and hands are relaxed at the finish.

Keep your head steady behind the ball at impact.

Do not tighten the grip pressure as you swing.

Your weight shifts across to the left side as your body turns.

Your belt buckle should point toward the target.

4 Allow your body to follow through and face the target. Hold your balance and watch the ball fly.

Allow your heel to come off the ground to ensure a full turn.

Swing for success
South Africa's Ernie Els possesses one of the smoothest swings in professional golf. His balance and poise provide a lesson to every golfer – never try to hit the ball too hard.

4 Unwind your shoulders and hips toward the target, releasing the energy created in the backswing. Let your hands and arms swing the club smoothly toward the ball.

The wrists are cocked, ready to hit the ball.

The lower body provides balance as you approach impact.

The shoulders unwind toward the target.

5 Look at the ball as you make contact and keep your grip steady. The force of the impact comes from your swing. Don't give it any extra push.

The right knee should bend in the direction of the ball.

Keep your head steady as you strike the ball.

The swing has been made with perfect balance.

6 Rotate with the momentum of the speeding clubhead. Finish with your weight supported on your left side and your knees together.

DOWNSWING

IMPACT

FOLLOW-THROUGH

Swing practice

WITH CONTINUAL PRACTICE, and the help of certain checkpoints, you can monitor your swing and repeat techniques to achieve consistency. As you get taller and stronger, the shape of your swing will naturally change, but if you are aware of the key steps, you can adapt your style as you grow.

2 Feel the connection between the club, your stomach, and your arms as you turn gently to the right.

The club must stay in contact with your belly button.

The takeaway

For a consistent swing, it is vital that your hands, arms, and body work together when you make your first move away from the ball. This drill will help you experience the sensation of a good takeaway, in which you turn your arms, stomach, and shoulders in a coordinated movement.

Use a mid-iron for this drill.

Make sure you have good posture at address.

Feel your body and the club work together as a unit.

1 Adopt your regular posture, but slide your hands down the shaft of the club until the butt end of the grip rests on your belly button.

The halfway back

Once you have moved the clubhead smoothly through the takeaway position, check your position at the halfway point. The shape of your swing as you work your way to the top is created by cocking your wrists. By the time your hands pass your right hip, the wrists should be fully cocked, and the clubshaft should be pointing toward the sky.

Make sure your wrists are fully cocked at the halfway stage.

Use a full-length mirror to check the progress of your swing.

At the top

From the halfway stage, turn the shoulders fully to the right to get to a good backswing position. Sense the muscles in your upper body stretching as you arrive at the top of your swing. Feel the momentum as you unwind your muscles in the downswing.

Turn your left shoulder under your chin.

Keep both knees flexed.

The lower body provides balance and stability.

3 Once you have rehearsed the drill several times, grip the club normally and try to re-create the same sensation as you make your takeaway. Keep the clubhead low to the ground as it moves away from the ball.

The clubhead follows a wide arc as it begins to swing.

Left-handed golfers
All golf instructions in this book are for right-handed golfers. Try holding a mirror alongside these pictures to see the left-handed positions.

Impact on a tire

You can experience what a good impact position feels like by setting up next to a firm object – like a tire. Press the clubhead firmly against it. Make sure that you use your whole body, not just your hands, to exert force on the tire.

Your head should remain steady.

1 Using a mid-iron, address the tire just as if you were addressing a ball. Grip the club in the normal way.

The wrists are firm and in control of the club.

2 Without making a swing, try to move the tire along the ground with the force of your body. Feel the clubshaft flex as you direct all your energy down through the club and into the tire.

The follow-through

When you unwind your swing, the momentum of the clubhead will pull your arms and body around to a full finish, so that your chest is facing the target and your weight is supported on your left side. Check the details of your follow-through in front of a mirror.

Your head rotates to follow the flight of the ball.

The clubshaft rests on your shirt collar.

Your hands and arms are relaxed at the finish.

Your right shoulder points toward the target.

Hold that pose!
To encourage good rhythm and balance in your swing, always try to hold your follow-through position for several seconds as you watch the ball fly toward the target.

The right knee turns in toward the left.

The right foot finishes up on the toe.

21

On the tee

Y OUR FIRST SHOT at each hole is taken
from the teeing ground. Longer holes, such
as fours and fives require you to drive the ball a
good distance from the tee. For these shots, use
a driver (the longest club) for teeing off, or, if
you are new to the game, you may find a 3-, 4-,
or 5-wood easier to use. For shorter holes, where
accuracy is more important than distance,
consider using a 3- or 4-iron.

Teeing
ground

*Markers on the teeing
ground indicate where
you should tee off.*

*Look at the ball,
but keep your chin
off your chest.*

*To establish good
width, swing your
left arm right
across your chest.*

Height of the ball
By placing the ball on a plastic
or wooden tee, you will achieve
greater distance and accuracy.
Make sure the tee is set at the
correct height. As a general rule,
choose a tee that lifts the ball to
a height where half of the ball is
above the top of the clubface,
whatever club you are using.

Driving tips
The driver swing is unlike
most other swings, because
you sweep the ball off the
tee as the clubhead begins
its ascent. This will increase
the distance of the shot. To
achieve a good driver swing,
first set up correctly, then
work on maximizing the
width and the stretch in
your swing to generate
extra speed and power.

2 Keep the clubhead low to
the ground as you glide it
smoothly back from the ball.
Do this slowly so that you give
your body time to complete a
full backswing. Let your arms
swing right across your chest
to make your swing as wide
as possible.

Driver   *3-wood*

Clubs
Woods, such as the
driver and the 3-wood,
strike the ball farther
than irons. This is
because the clubhead
on woods is chunkier,
and the shaft is longer,
than that of irons.

1 When you use the
driver, stand up
tall, with your feet
spread slightly wider
than shoulder-width
apart. Place the ball
forward in your
stance, opposite the
inside of your left
heel, where it can
be struck as the club
begins its ascent.

*Bend forward from your hips
and keep your back straight.
Align your body and clubface
squarely to the target, and
bend your knees.*

*Place most of
your weight on
your right side.*

Position on the tee
Before placing the ball on the tee, think about where you want the ball to land. If there is a hazard on one side of the fairway, play from the same side on the tee, and angle your shot away from trouble.

Your hands should finish low, behind the neck.

With good balance, you should be able to hold your finish for several seconds.

Turn your shoulders fully to the right.

Feel your side muscles stretch as you reach the top.

3 Complete the backswing by turning your upper body right around, away from the ball. Keep your right knee slightly bent and let your lower body resist the turning of your upper body. You should feel your body winding up like a spring.

4 As the body unwinds the club hits the ball at speed, sweeping it off the tee. Keep your arms straight through impact. Go with the momentum of the swing until you reach the finish position with your belt buckle pointing toward the target.

At the finish, your weight should be on your left side.

Keep your right knee flexed as your weight shifts across to the right side.

Driving for distance
The young American golfer, Tiger Woods, is an excellent driver of the ball. He has the suppleness, speed, and technique to hit the ball enormous distances.

Fairway strategy

ONCE YOU HAVE HIT the ball off the tee, you should assess the position, or lie, of the ball on the fairway or rough. If the ball is sitting on shorter grass on the fairway, play your next shot with a long iron or a fairway wood to gain distance. If the ball is lying poorly, for instance in long grass in the rough, concentrate on getting the ball into a useful position for the next shot. The secret to low scoring is not to take unnecessary risks but to let the lie of the ball dictate your strategy on the course.

Back on track
In really thick rough, playing for distance is simply not worth the risk – not even for a top professional. Here, twice Masters Champion José-María Olazábal opts for the shortest route back to the fairway.

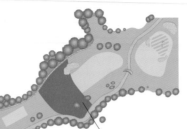

On this part of the fairway, strategy is an important part of the game.

Good lies and bad lies

The two players in this picture face two very different shots. The player on the left has found his ball in thick rough, while the player on the right's ball is sitting on a tuft of grass. In thick rough, it is best to focus on location, and use a lofted iron to make a high, short shot to get the ball safely back to the fairway. A good lie, such as a ball sitting on a tuft of grass, gives you the opportunity to be more aggressive with a long iron or fairway wood and to strike the ball a long distance toward the green.

Lofted iron (7-, 8-, or 9- iron)

Fairway wood (3-, 5-, or 7-wood)

Clubs

The worse the lie, the more lofted the club you should use. A good lie enables you to use a long iron or fairway wood and to be more aggressive.

The player on the right has a good lie and uses his yardage chart to establish how far he has to reach the green.

The player on the left has found a poor lie and checks his yardage chart to plan a safe escape back to the fairway.

Lofted iron for safety

Once you have decided to play for position with a lofted iron, focus on your target area and concentrate on making a good swing. Long grass tends to wrap itself around the club, which can cause the ball to fly off-line. To combat this, grip a little tighter than normal with your left hand.

1 Keep your lower body still as you turn your shoulders into the swing. The wrists should be fully cocked at the top of the swing, ready to add a little extra punch at impact.

2 To make solid contact with the ball, strike through the ball and the long grass. Keep your left-hand grip firm through impact.

Make it your priority to get the ball safely back in play.

3 While you need to be fairly aggressive to escape long grass, you must also keep your swing under control. A steady finish is a sign that your swing has been made with the balance necessary to achieve solid impact.

Fairway woods for distance

If you find your ball sitting on a tuft of grass, use a fairway wood (3-, 5-, or 7-wood) and go for distance. These clubs are much easier to hit with than long irons and are particularly effective on long par-4 and par-5 holes.

1 To play a good fairway wood shot, you need to make a wide swing. To make a wide swing, focus on keeping your left arm straight as you make a full shoulder turn.

2 As you accelerate smoothly through impact, sweep the ball cleanly off the turf. Keep your right arm fully extended as you swing the clubhead toward the target.

The ball should travel a good distance toward the green.

3 The momentum of your swing helps you all the way to the finish. The club should be draped behind your back, your eyes forward, and your body perfectly balanced.

Approaching the green

A S YOU APPROACH THE GREEN from the fairway, you need to have a well-thought-out strategy. Concentration is important here. You are aiming to land the ball as close to the hole as possible, but at the same time you must always be conscious of hazards (trouble) lurking around the green waiting to capture a wayward shot.

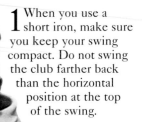

Approach shots are made 50–150 yd from the green.

Mental strategy

Use a yardage chart to calculate the distance to the green and to identify any potential hazards. The yardage information will help you choose the correct club and visualize the perfect shot in your mind's eye.

1 Check your yardage chart for distances and hazards. Opt to play for the safe side of the green, away from hazards.

Take care to aim the clubface at your target.

2 Once you have an image in your mind of where you want the ball to go, walk up to the ball and aim the leading edge of the club squarely along the target line.

Turn your head to check your target.

3 Settle your body into position over the ball, taking another good look at the target, until you are satisfied with your alignment.

Iron play

Select middle to short irons for these precision shots. Remember that iron play is all about accuracy of the strike, not the distance you hit the ball. The more ease you have when you swing the club, the better you will strike the ball. This 9-iron sequence illustrates the rhythm and control you should aim to achieve.

7-iron   9-iron

Clubs

Middle to short irons include the lofted 6-, 7-, 8-, and 9-clubs. They are played toward the middle of your stance. Apply a normal grip, but you may want to leave an inch or two of the shaft protruding at the top, to give you more control.

1 When you use a short iron, make sure you keep your swing compact. Do not swing the club farther back than the horizontal position at the top of the swing.

Your left arm creates the radius of your swing.

Keep the lower body passive as the upper body turns.

Practice distances

To make effective use of a yardage chart you need to know how far you can hit the ball with every club in the bag. When you practice, do as professionals do, and use the yardage markers on the range to help you calculate the average distance you carry the ball with each club.

Left-handed golfers
All golf instructions in this book are for right-handed golfers. Try holding a mirror alongside these pictures to see the left-handed positions.

Nick Faldo aims his shots at yardage markers to see how far he is carrying the ball with different clubs.

Keep your head just behind the ball at impact.

Let your head turn around naturally.

Visualize your shot
Jack Nicklaus once said that he never hit a shot until he had a vivid image of exactly what he intended to do with the ball fixed in his mind. He called this visualization of the shot "going to the movies."

Swing smoothly to make accurate contact with the ball.

The wrists are firm and in control of the club as it meets the ball.

Keep your back straight to prevent injury.

2 Because the ball is back toward the middle of your stance, the clubface hits the ball as the club is descending, and may take a small divot out of the ground. Don't force the shot – let the club loft the ball into the air.

3 The grace of your follow-through will reflect the control and the balance of the swing. Let your head come around naturally as you turn to watch the ball carry toward the target.

The knees come together at the finish.

Pitching

A PITCH SHOT is a high ball played with a lofted club, such as a pitching wedge or a sand iron. It is most effective from within 60–70 yards of the green. The aim of pitching is to carry the ball over rough and hazards and to land it softly by the flag, with the least amount of roll. It is worth practicing these pitch shots regularly, because they can really improve your final score.

Clubs
You can use either your pitching wedge or sand iron to play pitch shots. Experiment with these clubs to establish your favorite pitching distance with each one.

Pitching wedge   *Sand iron*

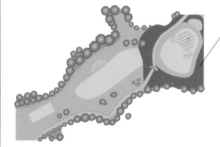

Pitch the ball from within 60–70 yd of the green.

Pitch shot

Pitch shots are played with a short, compact swing. Aim to cock your wrists early in your swing, to create a steep backswing. This produces a reverse spin of the ball, or backspin, which causes the ball to stop quickly when it reaches the ground. A good pitch shot will stop close enough to the hole to make only one putt necessary to sink the ball.

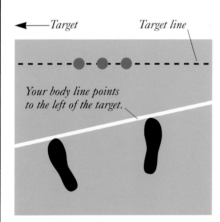

← *Target*   *Target line*

Your body line points to the left of the target.

Open stance
You need a slightly open stance at the address for a pitch shot. Place your left foot farther back than your right foot, so that your body is aligned slightly to the left of the target. The diagram shows a range of ball positions: The higher you want the shot, the farther forward (nearer the target) you place the ball.

As the wrists cock, the clubhead points up toward the sky.

Turn your back on the target.

Your left arm should swing across your chest.

1 To play this shot, take a slightly open stance. Aim the clubface at your target. Let your weight rest on your left side and position the ball toward the back of your stance. Your hands should be slightly ahead of the ball (nearer to the target).

Flex your knees for balance.

2 Make a steep, narrow backswing with little wrist cock. Don't move your lower body; your weight should remain where it was at address.

Lift the club right above your shoulder as you follow through.

Ball-turf impact
In this photograph, José-María Olazábal shows us a perfect example of the aggressive action needed to make a good pitch shot.

Keep your head steady as you release the shot.

3 Strike down and through the ball with force to create "ball-turf" impact. This contact causes a backspin, which stops the ball from rolling too far on the green.

4 The follow-through should reflect the control that you have maintained throughout the swing. Aim to make your finish the same length as the backswing.

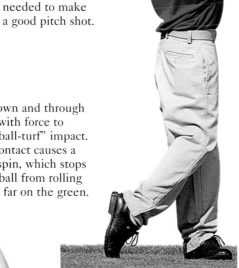

Pitching practice

Practice pitching regularly to increase your repertoire of shots. You can adjust the height of your shots by moving the ball position within your stance. Play it farther forward to hit the ball high and farther back to punch it low.

1 To develop your feel for distance, practice hitting shots 25–50 yards from the hole. Grip 1 inch or so down the club for a greater sense of control.

2 When you make your backswing, a useful thought to have is that of simply turning your chest away from the target. For short pitch shots, make your shoulder pivot quite small.

3 Keep your hands and arms relaxed as you unwind your body and swing smoothly through the ball. With practice you will develop the ball-turf impact that creates backspin.

4 Concentrate on making your follow-through the same length as the backswing. This will help you to accelerate through the shot. Hold your finish as you watch the ball fly toward the target.

Chipping

THE CHIP SHOT is used around the green to loft the ball and get it running toward the hole. It is a simple but versatile stroke that produces shots of varying height and length according to the club you choose to use. When you practice, it is important to experiment with a variety of clubs to develop a range of scoring shots. If your ball is resting on the fringe of the green, use a chip-putt shot to loft it over the fringe and on toward the hole. This stroke also uses a lofted iron.

Chip shots are taken 15 yd or so from the edge of the green.

The chip-putt

The chip-putt is really an extension of a long putting stroke (see pp. 34–5). It is a very useful (and a very safe) shot to play when the ball lies just a yard or so off the edge of the green. With a simple pendulum-type stroke (see p. 34) you can produce a shot that lifts the ball over the fringe and onto the green, where it runs toward the hole just like a putt.

Chip shot

The secret to good chipping is to take up the impact position at address. You can remind yourself of this by thinking "ball back, hands forward, weight forward" as you get ready to play. Once you have pre-set a good impact position, you create the chip shot with a gentle rocking of the shoulders and upper body.

1 Set up with an open stance – with your left foot slightly behind the ball-to-target line, so that you are aiming to the left of the target. Your feet should be fairly close together.

2 Gently rock your shoulders and upper body away from the ball. Let your hands and wrists respond naturally, keeping the clubhead low to the ground as it moves.

7-iron   9-iron

Clubs
Practice with different irons to develop a range of chip shots. The less lofted the club (a 7-iron, for instance), the lower the ball flies and the more it will run on the green. A more lofted club, such as a 9-iron, produces more height and results in less run of the ball.

Keep your eyes fixed on the back of the ball.

1 To start the chip-putt, grip well down the shaft of the club and play the ball well back in your stance, toward your right toe. Use a putting grip (see pp. 34–35) and make sure your hands are ahead of the ball.

2 Make a simple rocking stroke with your hands and arms. The club stays low to the ground and travels only 3 ft or so in the backswing. Keep your hands still through the stroke.

3 Let the club swing smoothly toward the target and clip the ball into the air. The angles between the club, arms, and shoulders should remain constant throughout.

Chipping over bunkers
If you are placed near a bunker close to the green, you will need to chip over it and stop the ball quickly. Use a sand wedge for this type of shot. To chip over uneven ground in front of the green, use a 7-, 8-, or 9-iron.

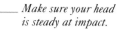

Make sure your head is steady at impact.

Your hands return to the position that they held at address.

3 At impact, keep your hands passive as the upper body turns toward the target and the ball is struck off the turf. A slightly descending blow helps you pitch the ball forward.

4 Your follow-through should be short and controlled. Keep your eyes on the ball and watch the shot unfold, just as you pictured it. The ball will land on your chosen spot, and should run to the hole.

Keep your lower body still.

Bunker play

L URKING BY THE FAIRWAY and around the green are sand traps, or bunkers. For a beginner, shots from bunkers can be awkward, but with practice and an understanding of the basic technique, they cease to be a problem. To play from a bunker you need a sand iron – a club especially designed to help the clubhead skim through the sand and "splash" the ball out of the bunker.

Sand irons

The sand iron (wedge) was invented by golfing great Gene Sarazen. It has a thick sole (flange) on the bottom of the club. The flange acts as a rudder, enabling the club to bounce off the sand rather than dig into it.

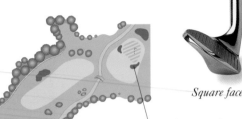

Flange

Square face   *Open face*

Bunkers are often found around the green.

Bunker shots

Normal golf shots need clean contact between the clubface and the ball. Bunker shots are unique in that the clubface does not actually touch the ball. The clubface strikes the sand 1–2 inches behind the ball and slides through the sand just under the surface. This produces a cushion of sand on the clubface that propels the ball up and out of the bunker. To achieve this, you need to make sure that the clubface is open at address (see above).

The wrists should cock early in a bunker shot.

Distance
The distance you fly the ball will depend on the length of your swing and the amount of sand you take from beneath the ball. The less sand you take, the farther the ball will carry. Practice will help you to get this right.

1 To compensate for the open clubface, which aims slightly right of the target, play with an open stance, so that the imaginary line across your feet points to the left of the target. Play the ball forward in your stance, with your weight evenly distributed.

2 Golf rules do not allow the clubhead to touch the sand at address, so hover the clubhead above the sand. Once you have set up correctly, swing along the line of your toes, and let your wrists cock early to create a flowing movement.

Open face

To make the most of the design of the sand iron, adjust the grip to open the clubface. As a general rule, the softer the sand and the more height you want on the shot, the more you need to open the clubface.

1 With just your left hand on the grip, swivel the clubshaft through your fingers until the clubface is turned a few degrees to the right.

2 Once you have opened the clubface, bring in the right hand and complete your grip as normal.

Upslope

Regardless of the ball's position in the bunker, always hit the sand rather than the ball. On a sloping lie, you need to get your shoulders parallel to the slope at address, and then swing normally. Here, Sweden's Per Ulrik Johansson rests his weight on his back foot and thumps the clubhead into the sand behind the ball.

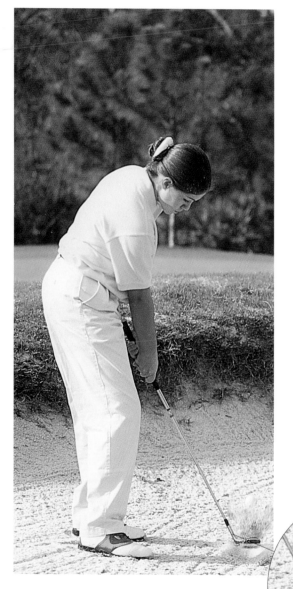

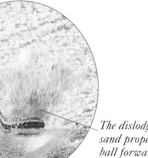

3 Focus on a spot 1–2 inches behind the ball and don't be afraid of hitting the sand quite hard. The momentum of your swing will be absorbed by the sand at impact, so you need to swing forcefully to make the ball travel only a small distance.

4 To swing with good rhythm, aim to make your follow-through at least the same length as the backswing. This will encourage you to accelerate the club through the sand. Keep your legs still and your feet firmly anchored to the bunker to stabilize your movement.

The dislodged sand propels the ball forward.

Putting

Putting green
The grass on the putting green is cut very closely to enable the ball to run fast and accurately. Greens range in size and have gentle slopes. Typically, they are surrounded by two or three bunkers.

THE OBJECT OF GOLF is to get the ball into the hole in as few strokes as possible. And, no matter how well you strike the ball from tee to green, your ability to do that rests with the quality of your putting – the act of rolling the ball into the hole. Experienced golfers spend more time practicing their skills with the putter than any other club in the bag.

Putting grip

Putting requires a special grip. You need a hold on the club that enables your hands to control the path of the putter. The most common grip is known as the reverse-overlap.

1 Hold the putter high in the palm of the left hand. This helps keep the left wrist firm during the stroke. When you close the hand, the left thumb should sit on top of the shaft.

The pendulum stroke

The basic putting movement that good players work on is known as the "pendulum" stroke. The hands and wrists should remain still while the action comes from the shoulders. Gently rock the arms back and forth to produce a smooth and controlled stroke.

1 Spread your feet apart, bend forward from the hips, and let your arms hang. Rest the upper part of each arm lightly on your chest – this establishes a good connection between club, arms, and your body.

Your hands should be slightly ahead of the ball at address.

Position the ball just forward of center in your stance.

Good alignment is critical. Make sure that your body is parallel to the line of the putt and that your eyes are directly over the ball. In the correct position you should find that you can swivel your head and see the line of the putt all the way to the hole.

For accuracy, keep your head still.

2 Your arms and shoulders work together as a unit to set the stroke in motion, while the hands and wrists remain still as the putter is drawn smoothly away from the ball.

The putter-head remains low to the ground.

Large mallet-headed *Mallet-headed* *Straight heel-toe* *Flanged blade* *Offset heel-toe*

Different putters
There are a wide variety of putters. Experiment with the various styles until you find a putter that both looks good and feels right when you place it behind the ball.

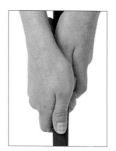

2 As you bring in the right hand, make sure that the fleshy pad at the base of your right thumb covers the left thumb. The fingers wrap themselves around the shaft to make the grip secure.

3 To form the reverse-overlap grip, drape your left forefinger across the fingers of the right hand. This locks the hands together, and gives you a good sense of control.

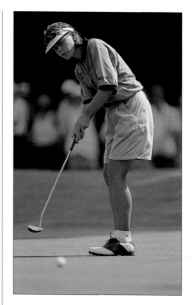

Perfect putting
Sweden's Annika Sorenstam displays a perfect finish, holding a balanced follow-through as she slowly turns her head to watch the ball roll toward the hole.

Steady address
Try suspending the putter-head just above the ground at address. Some players believe this helps eliminate tension.

The triangle created between the arms and shoulders keeps its shape throughout the stroke.

3 Your arms and shoulders continue to work together to produce a stroke through the ball. Let the putter accelerate through impact to set the ball rolling toward the hole.

The left wrist is firm, guiding the putter-head along the line.

Your feet and legs should remain still throughout the stroke.

4 The longer you can resist looking up to follow the ball, the better are your chances of success. Many putts are poorly struck when the player looks up too quickly. Keep your body still to prevent any jerky movement.

Playing the ball forward in your stance encourages a slightly ascending strike at impact, which gives the ball a true roll on the green.

Putting drills

ONCE YOU UNDERSTAND the basic principles of putting, you can develop your touch on the green by working on a number of putting drills. These exercises help focus your mind on the task of making your stroke and rolling the ball toward the hole. Remember, good putting is critical to good scoring, so practice regularly.

Practice with a friend

Competition sharpens your instincts on the green. When you practice with a friend, add a little pressure by competing between the holes. Take different ends, and putt one ball each, back and forth. Every time a putt is holed a point is scored. Play until one player has scored five, and then change ends.

Check your alignment

Short putts are often missed because of a basic error in the setup. So it is important that you keep a close eye on the alignment of the putter. When you practice, line up a short, straight putt and ask a friend to make sure you are aiming the putter correctly. You can then return the favor.

Ask a friend to check your aim.

The putter must be squarely aligned at address.

Aim to roll the ball into the back of the hole.

Circle the hole

Confidence is the key to making good putts and to repeating them under pressure. You can gain confidence by practicing from within about 3–4 feet of the hole. Practice by placing four or five balls in a circle around the hole, and knocking them in one by one.

Align the ball

Aim the manufacturer's name printed on the ball along the line of the putt. This will help you align your body and the putter-face square to the line of the putt, as demonstrated here by South Africa's David Frost.

Measure the length of your stroke to match the length of each putt.

Learn to read putts

Very few greens are completely flat, so you need to aim to the left or the right to allow for any curvature caused by sideslopes. The amount you need to allow is called the "borrow." The line you choose also depends on how hard you intend to hit the putt: The harder you hit, the less the ball will change direction, or break. Find a sloping green and practice approach putts from 30–40 feet. With experience you will learn how to read subtle breaks on the green and to judge the pace at which to roll the ball.

Distance control

To develop your feel for distance, pick out three holes on the practice green that give you putts of 20, 30, and 40 feet. Putt to each of them at random. The length of your stroke should control the distance the ball rolls – a relatively long putt requires a long stroke, and a shorter putt requires a shorter stroke.

Accuracy drill

Accuracy is the key to successful short putts up to 3–5 feet from the hole. This easy drill helps you feel the correct movement of the putter when you make short strokes. You can rehearse this stroke on both the putting green and at home on the carpet.

1 Form a channel by placing two clubs on the ground, parallel to each other. Take your set up position, making sure your feet, hips, and shoulders are square to the channel. Then work at short, precise strokes, keeping the putter within the two clubs.

Make a short, controlled stroke, and keep your eyes on the ball.

2 Think about the rhythm of your stroke as you accelerate "through" the ball. The putter should be square to the line of your putt when you complete the stroke.

Glide the putter through impact and roll the ball at your target.

Trouble shots

EVEN THE GREATEST players find themselves in trouble on the course sometimes. When faced with bad lies, they adapt their basic technique to get back on track. To develop escape shots, you need a vivid imagination and a desire to learn. When you practice, challenge yourself to play a range of difficult shots and improvise your way out of trouble. You will soon find that your all-around ball control improves.

High shots

If you play on a tree-lined course, there is a good chance that you will face a shot like this one, where trees stand between you and your target. This usually means that you have to fly the ball over the trees. To play this sort of shot, you need to make a couple of adjustments at address, and then make a normal swing.

Ball spin
Anytime you set up to play a high shot, remember that the spin you put on the ball will cause it to fly from left to right. Remember this when you take your aim.

1 Play the ball farther forward than you would normally. In this picture, a pitching wedge is positioned opposite the inside of the left heel. Your stance should be slightly open, with most of your weight on your right foot.

Safe water shots
If your ball lands in water, make sure you ascertain the depth of the water hazard before you try to retrieve the ball. Also, find out whether there are large stones under the water – it may be dangerous to walk on them.

Making a splash
Usually, when your ball disappears into a water hazard you have to declare it unplayable and take a penalty drop. A penalty drop in this case would mean dropping the ball on the grass on the edge of the water, which is counted as a shot. However, if you find your ball lying in shallow water, and part of it is visible above the surface, you can play the ball in a way that is similar to a bunker shot. Here, Payne Stewart hits into the water in a valiant attempt to propel the ball into the air.

2 Keep your weight on your right foot as you make your normal backswing. From here, concentrate on getting your weight under the shot and sliding the clubface beneath the ball as you accelerate through the sand.

3 Do not try to lift the ball into the air. The forward position will increase the effective loft of the club, which will automatically give you a high shot.

4 Aim to finish with your upper body slightly arched away from the target. A balanced follow-through reflects the nature of the shot you intended to hit.

Plugged lie

Opening the face of the sand iron and making a U-shaped swing is adequate for most bunker shots. But when the ball is plugged (buried in sand), you need to use a different technique to dig the leading edge of the club beneath the ball. You do this by adjusting your setup.

The clubhead should point to the sky.

Keep your body weight centered over the ball.

Make sure you are parallel to the target line.

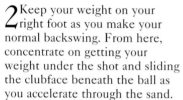

1 Set up with the clubface and your stance square to the line of the shot. Play the ball from the middle of your stance.

2 Aim to strike the sand 1 inch behind the ball. Make a steep, U-shaped swing, cocking your wrists sharply on the backswing.

Make sure the clubface is facing the target.

3 Thump the leading edge of the club into the sand 1 inch behind the ball. Blast the ball out with an explosion of sand.

Ballesteros adapts his swing to make a low shot.

Seve Ballesteros

Spain's Seve Ballesteros plays a low shot from under a tree. He bends very low on his knees to avoid swinging into the branches above.

Playing in bad weather

EVER-CHANGING WEATHER conditions add another challenge to the game of golf. You have to cope with wind, which can blow your ball off course, and rain, which can affect your grip. All golfers prefer to play under sunny skies, but if you equip yourself correctly and make allowances for poor weather, you can still have a lot of fun.

Wales's Ian Woosnam takes shelter while preparing for his next shot.

The caddie

A good caddie is essential to professional players – particularly in the rain. A caddie's job is to make sure that the clubs are clean and dry, and that the player is protected from the elements.

A wide umbrella prevents you and your equipment from getting too wet on the course.

A close-fitting woolen hat keeps you warm, but does not restrict your vision.

Tee seal

In very wet weather, put a tee in the hole at the top of each club's shaft before you put your clubs upside-down into your bag. This prevents rainwater from flooding the bottom of your bag.

Keep a towel handy for cleaning your clubs.

An all-weather, synthetic glove helps you maintain a good grip in the rain.

Bad-weather gear

If you are serious about playing golf, you may want to equip yourself with waterproof gear. This will enable you to play good golf while remaining relatively warm and dry. Most golfing manufacturers produce lightweight rain clothes specifically designed for the rigors of golf. They are often rustle-free, so that they do not distract you when you make a shot. It may be worth investing in some mittens or waterproof golf gloves, since you will need to keep your hands warm in order to make a relaxed grip. Take more than one pair on the course, in case the first pair gets soaking wet.

Waterproof clothing should be loose-fitting to enable freedom of movement in the swing.

Care of your equipment

In wet weather, your clubs are more likely to get dirty and wet. This not only damages expensive equipment, it also can stop you from playing effectively. Make sure you clean your clubs frequently.

Cleaning the grooves

The grooves on the face of the iron clubs are designed to grip and control the ball, so it is important to clean these grooves to keep them functioning properly. This is particularly true when the ground is soft and wet. Use the sharp end of a tee to remove dirt from the grooves.

Dry grip

Always check that the grip of your club and your hands are dry before taking a shot. Otherwise, the club will slip and you will lose control of the shot.

Handy towel

Wipe your clubface clean with a towel. Use a towel to keep your grips dry, too. When you return home from playing in wet weather make sure that you clean and dry your clubs and shoes.

Playing in the wind

A strong, gusty wind makes it difficult for you to maintain your balance and strike the ball solidly. Wearing rain clothes also tends to restrict your movement. To combat these adverse conditions, grip the club farther down than usual, and swing as smoothly and slowly as possible.

1 With all swings, place your feet a little wider apart than normal. Settle your weight evenly between the feet and play the ball toward the middle of your stance. This will help you to produce a low shot that flies under the wind so that it is not blown off course.

A wider than normal stance provides a firm base in windy conditions.

Shortening your grip enhances your control of the ball.

Waterproof clothing is essential in poor weather.

Keep the lower body steady.

Adjust your grip

In poor weather, you need to place your hands 2–3 inches farther down the club shaft than normal. Shortening your grip in this way gives you a greater sense of control and also helps you keep the ball low, under the wind.

2 Keep your lower body steady as you make a compact, three-quarter-length swing. The club should not reach a horizontal position at the top of the swing. Unwind smoothly through the ball to a controlled and balanced finish.

Teaching and practice

TO MAKE THE MOST of your natural talent for golf, you should take lessons and try to practice as often as possible. Regular instruction from a qualified Professional Golfers' Association teaching pro will help you avoid common pitfalls and reward you with a swing that will last you a lifetime. Contact your local club to find a pro who offers a program of junior instruction.

A teacher will use a video camera to record key movements in your swing.

Keep a record

Monitor your progress by writing notes every time you play golf. Comment on the accuracy of your drives and fairway shots, the success of your short-game skills around the green, and the number of putts that you take per round. This will help you assess which skills need the most practice.

Use a video camera

Visual feedback is a very valuable part of the learning process. With the help of a video camera, you can see how your golfing skills are progressing. You will be able to check your posture, and see any mistakes that you may be making as you swing. Most professionals use video to improve all aspects of their game – including putting.

A good teacher demonstrates and explains golf skills in simple terms.

Group lessons can be fun as well as effective because you can practice with partners.

Professional tip
You will achieve the best scores by improving your short-game skills. Spend at least half your practice time working on chipping, pitching, and putting.

Teaching pro

Ideally, you should find a reputable PGA teaching pro who will simplify the basics of the golf swing and will design an instruction program for you. A good pro will nurture your individual talent and provide you with practical drills and exercises that not only make learning the game fun, but speed your improvement.

Practice time

Remember that it's the quality and not the quantity of your practice that is important. Most golf clubs have practice ranges where you can work on your skills before progressing onto the course. Structure your practice time so that you work on all the skills of the game: driving, iron play, the short-game, and putting. As you improve, do as the top players do, and spend more time on the short game. You can practice with friends to add pressure and sharpen your competitive edge.

Teaching improves any player's technique and confidence.

Limber up

Always limber up before working on your game (see pp.12–13). It is just as important to warm up your muscles before a practice session as it is before a round of golf on the course.

Finalists at the Faldo Junior Series receive one-to-one teaching from the champion.

Top of the class

Each year, young British players compete in the Faldo Junior Series. One of the incentives to reach the finals is the opportunity to take lessons from the six-time major champion Nick Faldo. In this picture, Nick Faldo is passing on his knowledge of the swing to a lucky finalist.

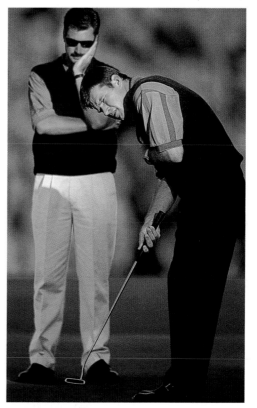

Even pros need a pro

It's not just beginners who need to take lessons. World-class players like Nick Faldo rely on a personal pro to monitor the consistency of their swing and to keep an eye out for any technical faults that may crop up from time to time. Remember, you will never stop learning, no matter how experienced you are.

Taking it further

A S ANY PROFESSIONAL golfer will tell you, the only way to improve your game is to practice and compete as often as possible. As you progress and gradually lower your handicap, you will find that you are up against more experienced players. You will need to perfect not only your technique but your mental toughness to play well under pressure. Only the very best make it to the pinnacle of the professional game, but everyone who plays golf can enjoy its challenges and rewards.

Youth competitions

Competition among other players in your age group helps your game and is a good way to make golfing friends. There is probably a "circuit" of junior tournaments in your area that will enable you to compete regularly, particularly through the summer months. Visit or call your local golf club to find out more about junior events.

Faldo Junior Series in Great Britain

Hard work and determination helped this young player to win against the competition in his age group at the finals of the Faldo Junior Series. Here, Nick Faldo and Prince Andrew – himself an avid single-figure golfer – present the trophy.

Tiger Woods played in his first PGA Tour event at the age of 16, and was ranked the world's No. 1 player at just 23.

Qualifying school

To qualify as a professional can involve attending a qualifying school, where several hundred players compete for just a handful of Tour cards each year so that they can play in the following year's tournaments. The "Q" school – as it is known – is a real test of nerve. Results are displayed on a large outdoor screen where players can see whether they have made the grade. Becoming a pro takes great talent and determination, and only the very best make it to the top.

Tiger Woods

Tiger Woods started playing golf at the age of three and is now one of the game's superstars. After winning three US Amateur Championships in a row, Tiger immediately made his mark on the professional game by winning the Masters in 1997. Tiger's great appeal has attracted young players around the world.

Major golf tournaments

THE MASTERS TOURNAMENT
Played every April at Augusta, Georgia, this tournament permits players to enter by invitation only and is a rite of spring for golfers.

THE US OPEN CHAMPIONSHIP
Held at a different course every June, it is open to amateurs as well as professionals.

THE BRITISH OPEN CHAMPIONSHIP
Always held in July on a great course, this is the oldest of the big four championships.

THE PGA CHAMPIONSHIP
Only open to professional players, this takes place at a different course every August.

THE RYDER CUP
A biennial tournament alternating between venues in the US and Europe, it is played over three days with foursome, four-ball, and single matches.

WOMEN'S US OPEN CHAMPIONSHIP
Primarily for women professionals, but amateurs can compete. Sites vary from year to year.

THE SOLHEIM CUP
Played on similar lines to the Ryder Cup, the Solheim Cup, inaugurated in 1990, is the premier women's professional team competition between players from the United States and Europe.

The Ryder Cup

This is the most famous team professional competition in golf. The first Ryder Cup match was played in 1927 as part of a biennial event to foster goodwill between British and American golfers. The US dominated the matches until 1977 when the British team was expanded to include European players. Here, Seve Ballesteros and his teammates celebrate victory in 1997.

Women's golf

In recent years women's professional golf has enjoyed a boom as more and more women and girls are attracted to the game. The majority of star players compete in the Ladies Professional Golf Association tour. Europe has produced a number of exceptionally talented players, such as Britain's Laura Davies and Sweden's Annika Sorenstam.

Young players like Britain's Johanna Head represent the future of women's golf.

The coveted British Amateur Championship trophy.

Sergio Garcia

Hailed by many as Europe's answer to Tiger Woods, Sergio Garcia of Spain won the British Amateur Championship in 1998 and the low amateur in the 1999 Masters Tournament.

Televised golf

The popularity of golf is reflected in the television coverage it receives. As well as the weekly Tour events, and the premier team competitions, there are a number of new World Golf Championships being played for enormous purses. These promise to bring together the world's greatest players on a regular basis, further fueling audience interest and attracting new players to the game.

Glossary

A

Address The starting position for a shot; also known as the setup. It involves the alignment of a player's body with the ball and target.

Alignment The direction in which the clubface and the body face at address or impact.

Approach shot Any shot toward the green from 50 to 150 yards away.

B

Backswing Part of the swing: the movement of the club away from the ball before it makes its downward swing toward the ball.

Baseball grip A method of gripping a club in which two hands rest unconnected on the grip.

Birdie The playing of a hole in one stroke under the par score.

Bogey A hole completed in one stroke over par. A double-bogey is a hole completed in two strokes over par and so on.

Boundary The outer limit of the golf course.

Bunker A hazard usually filled with sand around greens and sometimes on fairways.

C

Caddie A person who carries a player's clubs and equipment around the course.

Chip A short shot to the green.

Chip-putt A short shot to the green that is a combination of a chip shot and a putt.

D

Divot A piece of turf forced out of the ground by a clubhead after making contact with the ball.

Double-eagle The term used in the US for a score of three under par for a hole. In the UK this score is known as an albatross.

Downswing Part of the swing: the descending movement of the club after the backswing and before impact.

Driver The most powerful club, also known as the no.1 wood.

E

Eagle A hole played in two strokes under the par score for the hole.

F

Fairway The closely mown area of the course between the tee and the green.

Flange The thick sole on the bottom of a sand wedge.

Follow-through The finish position of the swing.

"Fore" The shout given by golfers to warn other players that a ball is heading in their direction.

Fringe or apron The area of grass surrounding the green. The grass is longer than on the green, but shorter than on the fairway.

G

Green The area of closely mown grass where the ball is putted into the hole.

Grip The part of the clubshaft held in the hands, usually covered with leather or rubber. Also means the grasp of the club made by the player.

Grooves The score lines on the hitting surface of a wood or iron.

H

Handicap The rating given to every player denoting the average difference between his or her score and the par for the course.

Hole The whole region between the tee and green; also the specific target in the ground. The hole has a diameter of 4¼ inches.

Hole out Completing the hole; putting into the cup on the green.

I

Impact The part of the swing when the clubface makes contact with the ball.

Interlocking grip A method of gripping the club in which the little finger of the right hand intertwines with the forefinger of the left hand (the opposite applies for a left-handed player).

Irons The clubs, numbered from 1-sand wedge, which are used for the majority of shots on the fairway and around the green. Iron clubheads are usually made of steel.

L

Lie The position of the ball on the ground; also the angle between the clubhead and the shaft.

Loft The angle of the slope of a clubface away from the shaft. The loft increases with the number of the iron, giving a higher shot with less distance.

M

Medal play A form of scoring in which the number of strokes a player takes to complete a round is compared with the other player's scores for a round. An alternative name for strokeplay.

N

Net score A player's score at the end of a round after deducting his or her handicap.

O

Open stance A stance in which the body line points to the left of the target (or to the right for left-handed golfers).

Out-of-bounds The areas of the course outside the boundary lines, usually marked by white stakes, ditches, or trees.

P

Par The score expected to be played by a first-class player for a hole, allowing two strokes on the green.

Pitch A high approach shot to the green.

Plugged A ball stuck in its own indentation in sand or soft ground.

Putt A short stroke played on the green with the aim of rolling the ball into the hole.

Putter A type of club used for putting.

R
Rough The area of unmown grass alongside the fairway that catches off-line shots.

Round The completion of all the holes on the course – usually 18 holes.

S
Sand wedge (or iron) An extremely lofted club with a wide flange designed for playing from bunkers.

Setup The address position, and the alignment of the body and the club to the target before making a shot; also known as the address.

Shaft The rod connecting the grip of the club to the clubface.

Sole The part of the clubhead that rests on the ground.

Spin The rotation of the ball after it has been hit hard.

Square stance A stance in which the line of your body (as in the position of your feet and shoulders) is parallel to the ball-to-target line.

Stableford A method of scoring based upon points per hole. For instance, if a player scores one over par, the player gets one point.

Stance The position a player adopts when addressing the ball.

Stroke index A system that shows the difficulty of each hole on a course.

Swing The continuous movement of the clubhead from the moment it leaves its address position, to the top of its backswing, down to impact, and on into the follow-through.

Swing path The direction in which the clubhead travels through the swing.

T
Takeaway Part of the swing: the first movement of the club from its address position as it starts its backswing.

Target line The imaginary line running through the ball to the target.

Tees The wooden pegs on which the ball is placed on the teeing ground. Also known as a tee-peg.

Teeing ground or tee A closely mown area from which the first stroke on a hole is played.

V
Vardon grip A method of gripping the club in which the little finger of the right hand overlaps the forefinger of the left hand (the opposite applies for left-handed players).

W
Waggle A smooth, back-and-forth wrist movement to relax muscles before the swing.

Wood A type of club used for longer shots. The clubhead may be made of wood or metal.

Useful addresses

American Junior Golf Association
2415 Steeplechase Lane
Roswell, GA 30076
770/998-4653
www.ajga.org

Ladies' Professional Golf Association
100 International Golf Drive
Daytona Beach, FL 32124-1092
904/274-6200
www.lpga.com

National Collegiate Athletic Association
P.O. Box 6222
Indianapolis, IN 46206-6222
317/917-6222
www.ncaa.org

The PGA of America
100 Avenue of the Champions, Box 109601
Palm Beach Gardens, FL 33410-9601
561/624-8400
www.pga.com

PGA Tour
112 PGA Tour Boulevard
Ponte Vedra, FL 32082
904/285-3700
www.pgatour.com

The United States Golf Association
P.O. Box 708
Far Hills, NJ 07931
908/234-2300
www.usga.org

Canadian Junior Golf Association
33 Gaby Court
Richmond Hill, Ontario
L4C 8X1
1-877-508-1069
www.cjga.com

Index

Acknowledgments

DK Publishing would like to thank the following people
for their kind help in the production of the book:

Special thanks to all the young golfers for their enthusiasm and patience during the photo shoots; Bowood Golf and Country Club for use of the course; Mizuno Corporation (UK), Reebok UK, Taylor Made Adidas, FootJoy, and Calloway for supplying golf equipment; Karl Shone for additional photography; Andy Komorowski for photographic assistance; Marcus James for design support; Hilary Bird for the index; Howard Cruthers, Caroline Greene, Clare Lister, and Penny York for editorial assistance; Mollie Gillard for additional picture research,

and Giles Powell-Smith for the jacket design.

Picture credits
The publisher would like to thank the following for their kind permission to reproduce their photographs:
a = above; c = center; b = below; l = left; r = right; t = top.
Action Plus: *44 tr;* Glyn Kirk *11 br;*
Allsport: *39 br;* Andrew Redington *23 br, 34 tr, 35 tr, 43 cr, 45 clb,* Andy Lyons *15 tr,* Dave Cannon *5 bc, 9 tr, 40 tr;* David Cannon *4 br, 5 br, 8 bl, 8 tr, 8 c, 8 bc, 9 tc, 19 tr, 29 tl, 43*

bc, 44 cl, 45 cr; Ken Levine *44 cr;* Paul Severn *7 tl,* Peter McEvoy *9 bc,* Rusty Jarrett *45 tr;* Simon Bruty *38 bl,* Stephen Munday *4 tr, 8 cl, 44 bl, 45 bc*
British Library: *5 tl*
Brown Brothers: *5 bc*
Colorsport: *33 tr*
Peter Dazeley: *4 c, 4 cr, 4 bl*
Hulton Getty: *5 clb*
Sotheby's Transparency Library: *5 tr*
Sporting Pictures (UK) Ltd: *24 tr.*
Endpapers: Peter Dazeley: *Matthew Harris.*

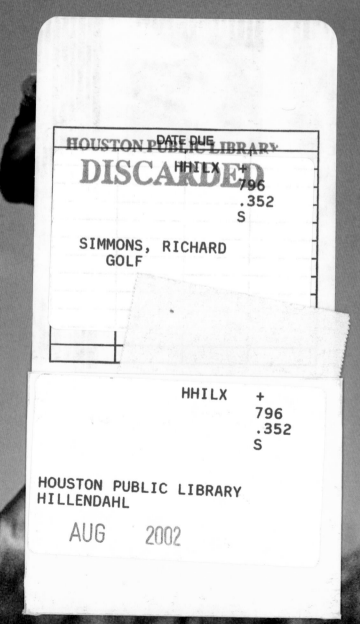